To:

From:

Associate Editor: Molly C. Detweiler
Assistant Editor: Heidi A. Carvella
Typesetting: Patricia Siemens
Project Manager: Patti Matthews
Design: Mark Veldheer

Printed in China
02 03 04/HK/ 4 3 2

JANUARY 1

Life is not a cup to be drained,
but a measure to be filled.

*Lord, you give [your people] drink from
your river of delights.*

PSALM 36:8

DECEMBER 31

Jesus Christ invested his life for you – have you shown any interest?

Jesus was chosen before the creation of the world, but was revealed in these last times for your sake.

1 PETER 1:20

JANUARY 2

Don't start today's work with yesterday's mud
on your feet.
Grandpa Fishback

*"Though your sins are like scarlet, they shall be as white
as snow," says the LORD.*

ISAIAH 1:18

DECEMBER 30

God will carry only those who allow him to carry them.

I, the Lord, have called you in righteousness; I will take hold of your hand. I will keep you.

ISAIAH 42:6

JANUARY 3

Use your mistakes as a guidepost, not as a hitching post.

If we confess our sins, God is faithful and just and will forgive us our sins and purify us with all unrighteousness.

1 JOHN 1:9

DECEMBER 29

The important thing is not so much where we stand as the direction in which we are going.

Whether you turn to the right or to the left, your ears will hear a voice behind you saying, "This is the way; walk in it."

ISAIAH 30:21

JANUARY 4

The truest expression of Christianity is not a sigh, but a song.

Let the word of Christ dwell in you richly … and sing psalms, hymns, and spiritual songs with gratitude in your hearts to God.

COLOSSIANS 3:16

DECEMBER 28

We often find true greatness in ourselves
when we're not actually looking for it!

*This is the one I esteem: he who is humble and contrite
in spirit," says the LORD.*

ISAIAH 66:2

JANUARY 5

A best friend is someone who is in your corner when you are cornered.

There is a friend who sticks closer than a brother.

PROVERBS 18:24

DECEMBER 27

As you think, so you are; you make or mar
your own success.

A prudent man gives thought to his steps.

PROVERBS 14:15

JANUARY 6

Jesus: the Life only Heaven could give;
the Gift only a heart can receive.

It is with your heart that you believe and are justified.

ROMANS 10:10

DECEMBER 26

If there was ever a doubt of God's love,
the story of Jesus settles it forever.

This is how God showed his love among us:
He sent his one and only Son into the world that we
might live through him.

1 JOHN 4:9

JANUARY 7

You never hear the still, small voice when you are listening to the crowd.

After the earthquake came a fire, but the LORD was not in the fire. And after the fire came a gentle whisper.

I KINGS 19:12

DECEMBER 25

Christ's first advent brought us grace;
His second advent will bring us glory!

Christ will appear a second time, not to bear sin, but to
bring salvation to those who are waiting for him.

HEBREWS 9:28

JANUARY 8

Treasures in Heaven are laid up only as
treasures on earth are laid down.

For where your treasure is, there your heart will be also.

MATTHEW 6:21

DECEMBER 24

Jesus Christ – the light that knows no power failure.
Paul L. Powers

Jesus said, "I am the light of the world. Whoever follows me … will have the light of life."

JOHN 8:12

JANUARY 9

Prayer is: Thank-, Ask-, Listen-, Know-ing –
to God!

*"Call to me and I will answer you and tell you great and
unsearchable things that you do not know," says the LORD.*

JEREMIAH 33:3

DECEMBER 23

Every footstep in life trembles with possibilities; every mile is big with destiny.

My steps have held to your paths; my feet have not slipped, O LORD.

PSALM 17:5

JANUARY 10

No man can follow Christ and go astray.

May the God who gives endurance and encouragement give you a Spirit of unity among yourselves as you follow Christ Jesus.

ROMANS 15:5

DECEMBER 22

Home – a place where the small are great,
and the great are small.

*Jesus said, "He who is least among you all —
he is the greatest."*

LUKE 9:48

JANUARY 11

"Do it now" is more than a motto;
it's a way of life.

Now is the time of God's favor, now is the day of salvation.

2 CORINTHIANS 6:2

DECEMBER 21

Think less about your rights and more about your duties.

Jesus said, "Whoever finds his life will lose it, and whoever looses his life for my sake will find it."

MATTHEW 10:39

JANUARY 12

An honest salesperson is one who sells goods that don't come back, to customers who do.

We are sure that we have a clear conscience and desire to live honorably in every way.

HEBREWS 13:18

DECEMBER 20

He who labors as he prays lifts his heart to
God with his hands.
St. Bernard of Clairvaux

The desires of the diligent are fully satisfied.

PROVERBS 13:4

JANUARY 13

Your church may point you
to Heaven, but it cannot carry you there.

Who shall ascend into the hill of the LORD?
Who may stand in his holy place?
He who has clean hands and a pure heart.

PSALM 24:3–4

DECEMBER 19

It is good to be children sometimes, and never better than at Christmas, when its mighty Founder was a child Himself.
Charles Dickens

To us a child is born, to us a son is given. . . . And he will be called Wonderful Counselor, Mighty God.

ISAIAH 9:6

JANUARY 14

Salvation is free, but you have to ask for it.
Paul L. Powers

Ask and it will be given to you; seek and you will find.

LUKE 11:9

DECEMBER 18

The world is not a playground;
it is a schoolroom.

*Teach us to number our days aright that we may gain a
heart of wisdom.*

PSALM 90:12

JANUARY 15

Great souls have wills; feeble ones have only wishes.

Jesus said, "I am coming soon. Hold on to what you have, so that no one will take your crown."

REVELATION 3:11

DECEMBER 17

We stop forgiving others when Christ stops forgiving us.

Jesus said, "If [your brother] sins against you seven times in a day, and seven times comes back to you and says, 'I repent,' forgive him."

LUKE 17:4

JANUARY 16

One secret of happiness is not to do what you like, but to like what you do!

So I saw that there is nothing better for a man than to enjoy his work.

ECCLESIASTES 3:22

DECEMBER 16

There is no trait of character more enriching than simple humility.

Everyone who exalts himself will be humbled, and he who humbles himself will be exalted.

LUKE 14:11

JANUARY 17

When walking through the "valley of
shadows," remember, a shadow is cast by light.
H. K. Barclay

*Even though I walk through the valley of the shadow of
death, I will fear no evil, for you are with me, LORD.*

PSALM 23:4

DECEMBER 15

A happy memory is a hiding place for
"unforgotten treasures."

*Delight yourself in the LORD and he will give you the
desires of your heart.*

PSALM 37:4

JANUARY 18

He who harbors a grudge will miss the haven of happiness.

He who covers over an offense promotes love, but whoever repeats the matter separates close friends.

PROVERBS 17:9

DECEMBER 14

There is more power in the pulpit when there is more power in the pew.
Dr. S. Kerr

There are many parts, but one body . . . If one part is honored, every part rejoices with it.

1 CORINTHIANS 12:20, 26

JANUARY 19

Sympathy is a golden key that unlocks the hearts of others.

God has sent me to bind up the brokenhearted, ...
to comfort all who mourn.

ISAIAH 61:1,2

DECEMBER 13

The wealth of a man is the number of things
which he loves and blesses, and which he is
loved and blessed by.
Thomas Carlyle

Honor the Lord with your wealth ...
then your barns will be filled to overflowing.

PROVERBS 3:9, 10

JANUARY 20

When you study the Bible "hit or miss," you always miss more than you hit!

Jesus opened their minds so they could understand the Scriptures.

LUKE 24:45

DECEMBER 12

Christmas began in the heart of God.
It is complete only when it reaches the heart
of man.

*The virgin will be with child and will give birth to a
son, and they will call him Immanuel — which means
"God with us."*

MATTHEW 1:23

JANUARY 21

A man knows least the
influence of his own life.

*[Your generosity] is not only supplying the needs of God's
people but is also overflowing in many expressions of
thanks to God.*

2 CORINTHIANS 9:12

DECEMBER 11

Others will follow your footsteps more easily
than they will follow your advice.

Direct my footsteps according to your word, LORD.

PSALM 119:133

JANUARY 22

The greatest thing a man can do for his heavenly Father is to be kind to some of His other children.
Henry Drummond

Live in harmony with one another; be sympathetic, love as brothers, be compassionate and humble.

I PETER 3:8

DECEMBER 10

Any adult is fortunate who gets their disappointments early in life, because they can learn to start over again.

The one who trusts in Christ will never be put to shame.

ROMANS 9:33

JANUARY 23

Our prayer and God's mercy are like two buckets in a well; while the one ascends the other descends.
Mark Hopkins

Let us then approach the throne of grace with confidence, so that we may receive mercy and find grace to help us in our time of need.

HEBREWS 4:16

December 9

If our faith were greater,
our deeds would be larger.

*If you believe, you will receive
whatever you ask for in prayer.*

MATTHEW 21:22

JANUARY 24

Once formed, the habit of prayer becomes as
natural as breathing.

*Jesus told his disciples a parable to show them that they
should always pray and not give up.*

LUKE 18:1

DECEMBER 8

The secret of spiritual advance is true and complete openness to God.

Jesus said, "Whoever comes to me
I will never drive away."

JOHN 6:37

JANUARY 25

Many little things are of greater value than big things. Could a cup of water exist without each drop?

If you have faith as small as a mustard seed ... nothing will be impossible for you.

MATTHEW 17:20

December 7

Great results cannot be achieved all at once,
but as we walk – step by step.

*May the Lord direct your hearts into God's love and
Christ's perseverance.*

2 Thessalonians 3:5

JANUARY 26

Recipe for having beautiful children:
be a beautiful parent!

*I have never seen the righteous forsaken or their children
begging bread. They are always generous and lend freely;
their children will be blessed.*

PSALM 37:25–26

DECEMBER 6

Forget your mistakes, but remember what
they taught you.

*We know that in all things God works for the good of
those who love him, who have been called according to
his purpose.*

ROMANS 8:28

JANUARY 27

Many people repent of their sins by thanking God they aren't as wicked as their neighbors.

First clean the inside of the cup and dish, and then the outside also will be clean.

MATTHEW 23:26

DECEMBER 5

Tact: the ability to give someone a shot in the arm without them feeling the needle.

Serve one another in love.

GALATIANS 5:13

JANUARY 28

There is no limit to what can be accomplished
if it doesn't matter who gets the credit.
Paul L. Powers

*It is God who works in you to will and to act according
to his good purpose.*

PHILIPPIANS 2:13

DECEMBER 4

Trouble starts when we become our brother's keeper and cease to be his friend.

Each of you should look not only to your own interests, but to the interests of others. Your attitude should be the same as that of Christ Jesus.

PHILIPPIANS 2:4–5

JANUARY 29

You have created us for yourself, Lord, and our hearts cannot be stilled until they find rest in you.
St. Augustine

Come with me by yourselves to a quiet place and get some rest.

MARK 6:31

DECEMBER 3

With every rising of the sun, think of your life as just begun.

Because of the LORD's great love we are not consumed, for his compassions never fail. They are new every morning; great is your faithfulness, LORD.

LAMENTATIONS 3:22–23

JANUARY 30

There can be no rainbow unless it has rained.

The Lord knows the way that I take; when he has tested me, I will come forth as gold.

JOB 23:10

DECEMBER 2

With the last step of the race you cross the finishing line.

Do you know that in a race all the runners run, but only one gets the prize? Run in such a way as to get the prize.

1 CORINTHIANS 9:24

JANUARY 31

Today, did you put your faith to test or to rest?

I am not ashamed of the gospel because it is the power of God for the salvation of everyone who believes.

ROMANS 1:16

December 1

Where the footprints of God lead you,
the grace of God can keep you.

*The fear of the LORD is the beginning of wisdom; all
who follow his precepts have good understanding.*

PSALM 111:10

FEBRUARY 1

Man needs more than a new start, he needs a new heart.

"I will give [my people] and undivided heart and put a new spirit in them; I will remove from them their heart of stone and give them a heart of flesh," says the Lord.

EZEKIEL 11:19

NOVEMBER 30

Defeat may serve as well as victory to shake
the soul and let the glory out.

*But thanks be to God! He gives us the victory through
our Lord Jesus Christ.*

1 CORINTHIANS 15:57

FEBRUARY 2

A good Christian shows the way, knows the way and goes the way.

Jesus said, "I am the way and the truth and the life. No one comes to the Father except through me."

JOHN 14:6

NOVEMBER 29

Let us keep to Christ, and cling to Him, and hang on Him, so that no power can remove us.
Martin Luther

I am convinced that neither death nor life, neither angels nor demons, . . . neither height nor depth, nor anything else in all creation, will be able to separate us from the love of God that is in Christ Jesus our Lord.

ROMANS 8:38–39

FEBRUARY 3

It's a wise parent who knows how to encourage a child's hidden talent.

Do not exasperate your children; instead, bring them up in the training and instruction of the Lord.

EPHESIANS 6:4

NOVEMBER 28

Enthusiasm is the greatest business asset in the world.

The LORD has done great things for us, and we are filled with joy.

PSALM 126:3

FEBRUARY 4

The main reason given by our Lord for not worrying about the future is that it's completely in his hands.

Jesus said, "Do not let your hearts be troubled. Trust in God, trust also in me."

JOHN 14:1

NOVEMBER 27

Conversion to Christ makes saints out of sinners.

Therefore, if anyone is in Christ, he is a new creation; the old has gone, the new has come!

2 CORINTHIANS 5:17

FEBRUARY 5

Work that is cheerfully done is usually well done.

Whatever you do, work at it with all your heart, as working for the Lord, not for men, since you know that you will receive an inheritance from the Lord as a reward.

COLOSSIANS 3:23–24

NOVEMBER 26

If you find excuses for sin, your sin will never be excused.

Confess your sins to each other and pray for each other so that you may be healed.

JAMES 5:16

FEBRUARY 6

Prayer changes everything—including us!

"You will call upon me and come and pray to me, I will listen to you" says the LORD.

JEREMIAH 29:12

NOVEMBER 25

Clouds may cover the sunshine but they
cannot banish the sun.

*As long as the earth endures, seedtime and harvest,
cold and heat, summer and winter, day and night will
never cease.*

GENESIS 8:22

FEBRUARY 7

A good bridge between despair and hope is a good night's sleep.

Weeping may remain for a night, but rejoicing comes in the morning.

PSALM 30:5

NOVEMBER 24

Few people get dizzy from doing too many good turns.

Do not forget to do good and to share with others, for with such sacrifices God is pleased.

HEBREWS 13:15

FEBRUARY 8

The caves of sorrow have mines of diamonds.

*He who goes out weeping, carrying seed to sow, will
return with songs of joy, carrying sheaves with him.*

PSALM 126:6

NOVEMBER 23

Wherever the Spirit of the Lord sways a heart, there is a passion to serve.

Let us consider how we may spur one another on toward love and good deeds.

HEBREWS 10:24

FEBRUARY 9

A smooth sea never made a skillful sailor.

[Trials] have come so that your faith — of greater worth than gold — may be proved genuine and may result in praise, glory and honor when Jesus Christ is revealed.

1 PETER 1:7

NOVEMBER 22

Trust in God –
his promises are as solid as a rock.

*God alone is my rock and my salvation; he is my fortress,
I will not be shaken.*

PSALM 62:6

FEBRUARY 10

If at first you don't succeed—don't worry, a
lot of people are willing to tell you why.

*Plans fail for lack of counsel, but with many advisers
they succeed.*

PROVERBS 15:22

NOVEMBER 21

Becoming a Christian is letting the love of God
into your heart and soul.

*Jesus said, "Here I am! I stand at the door and knock.
If anyone hears my voice and opens the door, I will come
in and eat with him, and he with me."*

REVELATION 3:20

FEBRUARY 11

Child's prayer at camp: "Jesus, I'll come again, 'cos I like myself when I'm near you."
Paul L. Powers

Whoever humbles himself like this little child is the greatest in the kingdom of heaven.

MATTHEW 18:4

NOVEMBER 20

God sees tomorrow more clearly than we see yesterday.

[The Good Shepherd] calls his own sheep by name ...
he goes on ahead of them, and his sheep follow him
because they know his voice.

JOHN 10:3–4

FEBRUARY 12

If you are not fishing, you are not following.

"Come, follow me," Jesus said, *"and I will make you fishers of men."*

MATTHEW 4:19

NOVEMBER 19

When it comes to giving, some people stop at nothing!

Whoever sows generously will also reap generously.

2 CORINTHIANS 9:6

FEBRUARY 13

All God's testings have a purpose, someday
you will see the light. But for now just put
your trust in him; walk by faith, not by sight.

*Those who know your name will trust in you, for you,
LORD, have never forsaken those who seek you.*

PSALM 9:10

NOVEMBER 18

A true friend is like the shade of a great tree
in the noonday heat.

A friend loves at all times, and a brother is
born for adversity.

PROVERBS 17:17

FEBRUARY 14

Love is like a bank. The more you put in,
the more your interest grows.

*Love always protects, always trusts, always hopes,
always perseveres.*

1 CORINTHIANS 13:7

NOVEMBER 17

Diamonds are only chunks of coal that stuck
to their jobs.
Minnie Richard Smith

All hard work brings a profit.

PROVERBS 14:23

FEBRUARY 15

He that gives good advice, builds with one
hand; he that gives good counsel and
example, builds with both.
Francis Bacon

*A wise man's heart guides his mouth, and his lips
promote instruction.*

PROVERBS 16:23

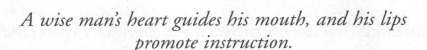

NOVEMBER 16

Well done is better than well said.

Jesus said, "You are my friends if you do what I command."

JOHN 15:14

FEBRUARY 16

God very often digs wells of joy with the spade of sorrow.

Jesus said, "Now is your time of grief, but I will see you again and you will rejoice, and no one will take away your joy."

JOHN 16:22

NOVEMBER 15

Treat people you meet each day as though it were your last day on earth.

Love one another deeply, from the heart.

1 PETER 1:22

FEBRUARY 17

Nothing is opened by mistake more often
than the mouth.
Paul L. Powers

*When words are many, sin is not absent, but he who
holds his tongue is wise. The tongue of the righteous is
choice silver.*

PROVERBS 10:19–20

NOVEMBER 14

Grudges, like babies, grow larger
when nursed.

*Live a life of love, just as Christ loved us and gave himself
up for us as a fragrant offering and sacrifice to God.*

EPHESIANS 5:2

FEBRUARY 18

No one, great or obscure, is untouched by
genuine kindness.

Jesus said, "I was a stranger and you invited me in."

MATTHEW 25:35

NOVEMBER 13

God has great confidence in you to place you where you are.

"I took you from the ends of the earth, from its farthest corners I called you. I said, 'You are my servant'; I have chosen you and have not rejected you," says the Lord.

ISAIAH 41:9

FEBRUARY 19

What our Lord did was done with this intent,
and this alone, that he might be with us and
we with him.
Meister Eckhart

*Jesus himself bore our sins in his body on the tree, so that
we might die to sins and live for righteousness.*

1 PETER 2:24

NOVEMBER 12

The soul would have no rainbow if the eyes
had no tears.
H. K. Barclay

*The Sovereign LORD will wipe away the tears from all
faces; he will remove the disgrace of his people from all
the earth.*

ISAIAH 25:8

FEBRUARY 20

In going out into the world, we often carry our "grief case" to do the daily work of the Lord.

Praise be to the Lord, to God our Savior, who daily bears our burdens.

Psalm 68:19

NOVEMBER 11

The little minutes, humble though they be,
Make the mighty ages of eternity.
Julia A. Fletcher

*There is a time for everything, and a season for every
activity under heaven.*

ECCLESIASTES 3:1

FEBRUARY 21

Keep your confidence in God and he'll keep
your cares.
H. K. Barclay

*The LORD will be your confidence and will keep your
foot from being snared.*

PROVERBS 3:26

NOVEMBER 10

When Christ prepares the table for us it is
always a well-balanced meal.
H. K. Barclay

*You prepare a table before me in the presence of my
enemies ... my cup overflows.*

PSALM 23:5

FEBRUARY 22

O God, make us children of quietness and
heirs of peace.
Clement of Rome

*In repentance and rest is your salvation, in quietness and
trust is your strength.*

ISAIAH 30:15

NOVEMBER 9

Patience carries a lot of wait!

Imitate those who through faith and patience inherit what has been promised.

HEBREWS 6:12

FEBRUARY 23

Be on the lookout for mercies. The more we look for them, the more of them we will see.

Be joyful always; pray continually; give thanks in all circumstances.

I THESSALONIANS 5:16-18

NOVEMBER 8

Christ helps us to face the music, even when
we don't like the tune.

When I am afraid, I will trust in you, LORD.

PSALM 56:3

FEBRUARY 24

You can't do much about your ancestors, but you can influence your descendants enormously.

Come, my children, listen to me; I will teach you the fear of the LORD.

PSALM 34:11

NOVEMBER 7

Joy is like a boomerang; the moment you fling it, it returns.

Give, and it will be given to you. A good measure, pressed down, shaken together and running over, will be poured into your lap.

LUKE 6:38

FEBRUARY 25

Love him totally who gave himself totally for
your love.
Claire of Assisi

*The life I live in body, I live by faith in the Son of God,
who loved me and gave himself for me.*

GALATIANS 2:20

NOVEMBER 6

God can do wonders with a broken heart if we give him all the pieces.

The LORD is close to the brokenhearted and saves those who are crushed in spirit.

PSALM 34:18

FEBRUARY 26

Prayer is not conquering God's reluctance,
but taking hold of God's willingness.
Phillips Brooks

*"My eyes will be open and my ears attentive to the
prayers offered in this place," says the LORD.*

2 CHRONICLES 7:15

NOVEMBER 5

The crowns we cast at Jesus' feet must all be won on earth.

Our light and momentary troubles are achieving for us an eternal glory that far outweighs them all.

2 CORINTHIANS 4:17

FEBRUARY 27

Friendship between the friends of Jesus is
unike any other friendhsip.
Stephen Neill

*Jesus said, "Where two or three come together in my name,
there am I with them."*

MATTHEW 18:20

NOVEMBER 4

The Christian's place is on the frontline, not
on the sideline.
Don Moowma

*We proclaim Jesus, admonishing and teaching everyone
with all wisdom, so that we may present everyone perfect
in Christ.*

COLOSSIANS 1:28

FEBRUARY 28

The fruit of the Christian is ripened in Sonshine!

Grow in the grace and knowledge of our Lord and Savior Jesus Christ.

2 PETER 3:18

NOVEMBER 3

There is a great chasm between books men
make and the Book
that makes men.

*As for God, his way is perfect; the word of the LORD is
flawless. He is a shield for all who take refuge in him.*

PSALM 18:30

FEBRUARY 29

In the Christian life, an ounce of truth is worth a ton of talk.

Let the wise listen and add to their learning.

PROVERBS 1:5

NOVEMBER 2

It is our joy and privilege to know Christ as
God's unspeakable gift.
Hudson Taylor

Thanks be to God for his indescribable gift!

2 CORINTHIANS 9:15

MARCH 1

Let your first "Good Morning" be to your
Father in heaven.
Karl G. Maeser

*Very early in the morning ... Jesus got up, left the house
and went off to a solitary place, where he prayed.*

MARK 1:35

NOVEMBER 1

The name of Jesus may be a byword to the sinner, but it is a password to Heaven for the saint.

Give him the name Jesus, because he will save his people from their sins.

MATTHEW 1:21

MARCH 2

You can't break God's promises by leaning on them!

Cast all your anxiety on God because he cares for you.

I PETER 5:7

OCTOBER 31

Thanksgiving is a good thing:
thanksliving is better.

*In God we make our boast all day long, and we will
praise your name forever.*

PSALM 44:8

MARCH 3

Angry at another's faults? Count ten –
of your own!

Better a patient man than a warrior.

PROVERBS 16:32

OCTOBER 30

Experience is yesterday's answer
to today's problem.

*How much better to get wisdom than gold, to choose
understanding rather than silver!*

PROVERBS 16:16

MARCH 4

Aim to carve your name on hearts,
not on marble.

*Come and listen, all you who fear God; let me tell you
what he has done for me.*

PSALM 66:16

OCTOBER 29

God's treasure house, the Bible, is unlocked
only by the golden key of meditation.

*I meditate on your precepts and consider your ways, O
Lord. I delight in your decrees; I will not
neglect your word.*

PSALM 119:15–16

MARCH 5

Scripture states the only thing we can demand of God is ... "thy will be done!"

I desire to do your will, O my God; your law is within my heart.

PSALM 40:8

OCTOBER 28

If you plan to build a tall house of virtues,
you must first lay deep foundations of
humility.
St. Augustine

A man of lowly spirit gains honor.

PROVERBS 29:23

MARCH 6

When God measures a man, He puts the tape around the heart instead of the head.

The LORD does not look at the things man looks at. Man looks at the outward appearance, but the LORD looks at the heart.

1 SAMUEL 16:7

OCTOBER 27

Everyone lives in one of two tents: con-tent or discon-tent.

I have learned the secret of being content in any and every situation. . . . I can do everything through Christ who gives me strength.

PHILLIPIANS 4:12–13

MARCH 7

The heart of a child is the most precious of
God's creation.
Joseph L. Whitten

*Train up a child in the way he should go, and when he is
old he will not turn from it.*

PROVERBS 23:6

OCTOBER 26

God gives us crosses in this life, so that we may wear crowns in the next.

Jesus said, "To him who overcomes, I will grant the right to sit with me on my throne, just as I overcame and sat down with my Father on his throne."

REVELATION 3:21

MARCH 8

The Bible is the only book whose Author is always present when it is read.

"I am the Alpha and the Omega," says the Lord God, "who is, and who was, and who is to come, the Almighty."

REVELATION 1:8

OCTOBER 25

It is better to forgive and forget than to resent and remember.

Forgive us our debts, as we also have forgiven our debtors.

MATTHEW 6:12

MARCH 9

We are all pencils in the hand of a writing God, who is sending love letters to the world.
Mother Teresa

Therefore, my dear brothers, stand firm. ...your labor in the Lord is not in vain.

I CORINTHIANS 15:58

OCTOBER 24

The texture of eternity is woven on the looms
of time on earth.

*Blessed are those who have not seen
and yet have believed.*

JOHN 20:29

MARCH 10

Take my will and make it Thine;
It shall be no longer mine.
Take my heart, it is Thine own;
It shall be Thy royal throne.
Frances Ridley Havergal

*God how began a good work in you will carry it on to
completion until the day of Jesus Christ.*

PHILIPPIANS 1:6

OCTOBER 23

Christ is like a river. A river is continually flowing, there are fresh supplies of water coming from the fountain-head continually, so that a man may live by it and be supplied with water all his life.

Jonathan Edwards

Jesus said, "If anyone is thirsty, let him come to me and drink. Whosoever believes in me, as the Scripture has said, streams of living water will flow from within him."

JOHN 7:37–38

MARCH 11

The purpose of Christianity is not to avoid
the difficulty, but to produce character
adequate to meet it when it comes.
James L. Christensen

*Suffering produces perseverance;
perseverance, character; and character, hope.*

ROMANS 5:3–4

OCTOBER 22

I have a great need for Christ; I have a great
Christ for my need.
C.H. Spurgeon

*My God will meet all your needs according to his glorious
riches in Christ Jesus.*

PHILIPPIANS 4:19

MARCH 12

A true missionary is God's child in God's place, doing God's work in God's way — for God's glory!

We fix our eyes not on what is seen, but on what is unseen. For what is seen is temporary, but what is unseen is eternal.

2 CORINTHIANS 4:18

OCTOBER 21

God does not comfort us to make us
comfortable, but to make us comforters.
J.H. Jowett

*Praise be to God and Father of our Lord Jesus Christ . . .
who comforts us in all our troubles, so that we can
comfort those in any trouble with the comfort we
ourselves have received from God.*

2 CORINTHIANS 1:3–4

MARCH 13

Some people fail to recognize opportunity because it comes disguised in work clothes.

Never tire of doing what is right.

2 THESSALONIANS 3:13

OCTOBER 20

Our love for God is best evident by our love to others.

Jesus said, "By this all men will know that you are my disciples, if you love one another."

JOHN 13:35

MARCH 14

Our duty is not to see through one another,
but to see one another through.

*Let us not give up meeting together, as some are in the
habit of doing, but let us encourage one another.*

HEBREWS 10:25

OCTOBER 19

Faithfulness in little things is a great thing.

Well done, good and faithful servant! You have been faithful with a few things; I will put you in charge of many things.

MATTHEW 25:21

MARCH 15

Be thankful if you have a job a little harder than you like – a razor can't be sharpened on a piece of velvet.

For Christ's sake, I delight in weaknesses, in insults, in hardships, in persecutions, in difficulties. For when I am weak, then I am strong.

2 Corinthians 12:10

OCTOBER 18

Salvation is not "try," but trust; not "do," but done!
Corrie Ten Boom

Whoever believes in the Son has eternal life.

JOHN 3:36

MARCH 16

Success comes in cans – failures in can'ts.

The God of heaven will give us success.

NEHEMIAH 2:20

OCTOBER 17

The most overloaded, desperate people are those who can see no other burdens but their own.

Carry each other's burdens, and in this way you will fulfill the law of Christ.

GALATIANS 6:2

MARCH 17

The poorest man is he whose only
wealth is money.
Dr. Leroy Gager

*Has not God chosen those who are poor in the eyes of the
world to be rich in faith and to inherit the kingdom he
promised those who love him?*

JAMES 2:5

OCTOBER 16

The best exercise for strengthening the heart
is reaching down and lifting people up.
Ernest Blevins

*Be kind and compassionate to one another, forgiving
each other, just as in Christ God forgave you.*

EPHESIANS 4:32

MARCH 18

To have an upright life, lean on Jesus.

Whosoever trusts in the LORD is kept safe.

PROVERBS 29:25

OCTOBER 15

Serving Christ under law is a duty, under love is a delight.

Never be lacking in zeal, but keep your spiritual fervor, serving the Lord.

ROMANS 12:11

MARCH 19

God gives the cross, and the cross gives us God.
Madame Guyon

*God forgave us all our sins, having canceled the written
code, with its regulations, that was against us and that
stood opposed to us; he took it away, nailing it to the cross.*

COLOSSIANS 2:13–14

OCTOBER 14

A sorrow shared is but half a trouble. But a joy that's shared is a joy made double!

If we are children, then we are heirs—heirs of God and co-heirs with Christ, if indeed we share in his sufferings in order that we may also share in his glory.

ROMANS 8:17

MARCH 20

The only haven of safety is in the mercy of God, as manifested in Christ, in whom every part of our salvation is complete.
John Calvin

You will go on your way in safety, and your foot will not stumble.

PROVERBS 3:23

OCTOBER 13

The first step to victory: recognize the enemy!

Put on the full armor of God so that you can take your stand against the devil's schemes.

EPHESIANS 6:11

MARCH 21

Even at the midnight hour, Christ wants us
to believe in his daylight.

*In the night I remember your name, O LORD, and will
keep your law.*

PSALM 119:55

OCTOBER 12

God can give only according to His might;
therefore He always gives more than
we ask for.
Martin Luther

*To God who is able to do immeasurably more than all
we ask or imagine, according to his power that is at work
within us, to him be glory in the church and in Christ
Jesus throughout all generations, for ever and ever! Amen.*

EPHESIANS 3:20–21

MARCH 22

I am responsible to God for the talent he has given me.

We have different gifts, according to the grace given us.

ROMANS 12:6

OCTOBER 11

We are judged by what we finish, not by what we start.
L. P. Powers

I have fought the good fight, I have finished the race, I have kept the faith.

2 TIMOTHY 4:7

MARCH 23

Contentment is a pearl of great price, and whoever procures it at the expense of ten thousand desires makes a wise and happy choice.
John Balguy

Godliness with contentment is great gain.

I TIMOTHY 6:6

OCTOBER 10

Where God guides, he provides!

The Lord makes me lie down in green pastures, he leads me beside quiet waters, he restores my soul. He guides me in paths of righteousness for his name's sake.

PSALM 23:2–3

MARCH 24

Let Christ work in you, then he will work through you.

*If Christ is in you . . . your spirit is alive
because of righteousness.*

ROMANS 8:10

OCTOBER 9

If we have pleasant thoughts, even when we
are alone, we are in good company.

I meditate on all your works and consider what
your hands have done, O LORD.

PSALM 143:5

MARCH 25

It is not the sense of God's presence but the
fact of his presence that is our strength.
F.B. Dixon

*You have made known to me the path of life, O Lord;
you will fill me with joy in your presence, with eternal
pleasures at your right hand.*

PSALM 16:11

OCTOBER 8

Spend your life any way you like, but
remember you can only spend it once!
Reverend Leroy Gager

Take hold of the life that is truly life.

1 TIMOTHY 6:19

MARCH 26

Surrounded by peace, no one is ever alone.

The God of peace will be with you.

PHILIPPIANS 4:9

OCTOBER 7

Live above the circumstances, not under them.

*Since, . . . you have been raised with Christ, set your
hearts on things above, where Christ is seated at the right
hand of God.*

COLOSSIANS 3:1

MARCH 27

Witnessing for Christ is not getting into the
mood but being in the mode.
Paula Powers

*The LORD said, "Whom shall I send? And who will go
for us?" And I said "Here am I. Send me!"*

ISAIAH 6:8

OCTOBER 6

Against wrong's own darkness comes the
welcome strength of right.

*You, O LORD, keep my lamp burning; my God turns my
darkness into light.*

PSALM 18:28

MARCH 28

Keep your light shining. God will put it
where it can be seen.

*Put your trust in the light while you have it, so that you
may become sons of the light.*

JOHN 12:36

OCTOBER 5

Before becoming an effective worker for the Lord, take time to study The Manual.

Jesus said, "I will give you words and wisdom that none of your adversaries will be able to resist or contradict."

LUKE 21:15

MARCH 29

God made our faces round; only we can make them long.

A happy heart makes the face cheerful.

PROVERBS 15:13

OCTOBER 4

We should not ignore our dreams. God will
sometimes use them to assure us
of his promises.
M. F. Powers

*"I will pour out my Spirit on all people. Your sons and
daughters will prophesy, your old men will dream
dreams, your young men will see visions," says the Lord.*

JOEL 2:28

MARCH 30

We cannot discover new seas unless we are prepared to leave the shore.

All these people [Abel, Noah, Enoch, Abraham] were still living by faith when they died. . . . And they admitted that they were aliens and strangers on earth. People who say such things show that they are looking for a country of their own.

HEBREWS 11:13–14

OCTOBER 3

Wherever we go, we cannot step outside the
boundaries of God's love and care.
M. F. Powers

*If I rise on the wings of the dawn, if I settle on the far
side of the sea, even there your hand will guide me, your
right hand will hold me fast, O Lord.*

PSALM 139:9–10

MARCH 31

Kind words do not cost much. Yet they accomplish much.
Blaise Pascal

An anxious heart weighs a man down, but a kind word cheers him up.

<small>PROVERBS 12:25</small>

OCTOBER 2

The Lord seeks men and women who are not ashamed to be seen down on their knees in prayer.

The eyes of the LORD range throughout the earth to strengthen those whose hearts are fully committed to him.

2 CHRONICLES 16:9

APRIL 1

Through the footprints of faith we see in Jesus everything that God is.

No one has seen God, but God the One and Only, who is at his Father's side, has made him known.

JOHN 1:18

OCTOBER 1

Faith unlocks the door to
ultimate achievement.

*Everyone born of God overcomes the world. . . . Who is it
that overcomes the world? Only he who believes that Jesus
is the Son of God.*

1 JOHN 5:4–5

APRIL 2

The confession of sinful work is the beginning of good works.

He who conceals his sins does not prosper, but whoever confesses and renounces them finds mercy.

PROVERBS 28:13

SEPTEMBER 30

I bless the Lord that all our troubles come
through Christ's fingers, and that he puts sugar
on them and puts the spirit of glory in our cup.
Samuel Rutherford

*The righteous cry out, and the LORD hears them; he
delivers them from all their troubles.*

PSALM 34:17

APRIL 3

It's no use trying to shine if you haven't taken
time to fill your lamp.

*God, who said, "Let light shine out of darkness," made his
light shine in our hearts to give us the light of the
knowledge of the glory of God in the face of Christ.*

2 CORINTHIANS 4:6

SEPTEMBER 29

When loneliness overtakes us, we need to remember that we are *not alone*. God has promised to be with us.
M. F. Powers

"When you pass through the waters, I will be with you; and when you pass through the rivers, they will not sweep over you," says the Lord.

ISAIAH 43:2

APRIL 4

A Christian heart delights to love –
without return.

We love because God first loved us.

1 JOHN 4:19

SEPTEMBER 28

Today's seed brings tomorrow's harvest.

Let us not become weary in doing good, for at the proper time we will reap a harvest if we do not give up.

GALATIANS 6:9

APRIL 5

His banner over us is love,
Our sword the Word of God.
We tread the road the saints above
With shouts of triumph trod.
John H. Yates

You give me your shield of victory; you stoop down to make me great, O LORD.

2 SAMUEL 22:36

SEPTEMBER 27

God is often more concerned about your response to the problem than he is in removing the problem.

My eyes are ever on the LORD, for only he will release my feet from the snare.

PSALM 25:15

APRIL 6

Man is really free only in God, the source of his freedom.
Sherwood Eddy

If the Son sets you free, you will be free indeed.

JOHN 8:36

SEPTEMBER 26

Happiness is where it is found, but seldom
where it is sought.
J. Billings

*To the man who pleases him, God gives wisdom,
knowledge and happiness.*

ECCLESIASTES 2:26

APRIL 7

To take care of oneself is the first law of nature,
but to deny oneself is the first law of grace.

*Jesus said, "If anyone would come after me, he must deny
himself and take up his cross and follow me."*

MARK 8:34

SEPTEMBER 25

Nothing is so strong as gentleness, nothing so
gentle as real strength.
Francis de Sales

Let your gentleness be evident to all.

PHILIPPIANS 4:5

APRIL 8

God does not give us everything we want, but
He does fulfill all His promises, leading us
along the best and straightest paths to Himself.
Dietrich Bonhoeffer

*Teach me to do your will, for you are my God; may your
good Spirit lead me on level ground.*

Psalm 143:10

SEPTEMBER 24

A friend is the first person to come in when others go out.

Greater love has no one than this, that he lay down his life for his friends.

JOHN 15:13

APRIL 9

Jesus Christ is not valued at all until he is valued above all.

God raised Christ from the dead and seated him at his right hand in the heavenly realms, far above all rule and authority, power and dominion, and every title that can be given, not only in the present age but also in the one to come.

EPHESIANS 1:20–21

SEPTEMBER 23

Repentant prayer is one weapon
Satan can't duplicate.

*Jesus said, "I tell you, there is rejoicing in the presence
of the angels of God over one sinner
who repents."*

LUKE 15:10

APRIL 10

You don't stop laughing because you grow old
– you grow old because you stop laughing.

A cheerful heart is a good medicine.

PROVERBS 17:22

SEPTEMBER 22

God loves us the way we are, but too much
to leave us that way.
Leighton Ford

*God demonstrates his own love for us in this: While we
were still sinners, Christ died for us.*

ROMANS 5:8

April 11

God doesn't mind our questions when we
come to him with a seeking heart. God is
bigger than any question we can ask.
M. F. Powers

*Why do you hold back your hand, your right hand? . . .
But you, O God, are my king from of old; you bring
salvation upon the earth.*

PSALM 74:11–12

SEPTEMBER 21

There is hope for all of us. There is light.
Jesus Christ, the Son of God, is our hope and
light in darkness.
M. F. Powers

*You are my lamp, O LORD; the LORD turns my darkness
into light.*

2 SAMUEL 22:29

APRIL 12

Christ's riches are unsearchable, and the gospel is the field this treasure is hidden in.
Thomas Goodwin

God raised us up with Christ and seated us with him in the heavenly realms in Christ Jesus, in order that in the coming ages he might show the incomparable riches of his grace, expressed in his kindness to us in Christ Jesus.

EPHESIANS 2:6–7

SEPTEMBER 20

Is your life a witness, with testimony true?
Could the world be won to Christ by what
others see in you?
Paul L. Powers

*Let your light shine before men, that they may see your
good deeds and praise your Father in heaven.*

MATTHEW 5:16

APRIL 13

Friendship, of itself a holy tie, is made more
sacred by adversity.
Charles Caleb Colton

A despairing man should have the devotion of his friends.

JOB 6:14

SEPTEMBER 19

The future is as bright as the
promises of God!
Adoniram Judson

*Not one of all the LORD's good promises to the house of
Israel failed; every one was fulfilled.*

JOSHUA 21:45

APRIL 14

Life is a succession of lessons, which must be lived to be understood.

Jesus said, "Take my yoke upon you and learn from me, for I am gentle and humble in heart, and you will find rest for your souls."

MATTHEW 11:29

SEPTEMBER 18

Kindness has converted more sinners than zeal, eloquence or learning.

How beautiful are the feet of those who bring good news!

ROMANS 10:15

APRIL 15

Pray believing, have faith and then trust!
Dr. Ernest Meyers

Trust in the Lord with all your heart.

PROVERBS 3:5

SEPTEMBER 17

The first thing about wisdom is to know the truth; the second is to discern what is false.
J. Lake

Surely you desire truth in the inner parts, Lord; you teach me wisdom in the inmost place.

PSALM 51:6

APRIL 16

Never borrow sorrow from tomorrow.

Jesus said, "Do not worry about tomorrow, for tomorrow will worry about itself. Each day has enough trouble of its own."

MATTHEW 6:34

SEPTEMBER 16

Grant that I may not pray alone with the
mouth; help me that I may pray from the
depths of my heart.
Martin Luther

Pray in the Spirit on all occasions.

EPHESIANS 6:18

APRIL 17

Remember that the sign on the door to opportunity reads: push.

Pray ... that God may open a door for our message, so that we may proclaim the mystery of Christ.

COLOSSIANS 4:3

SEPTEMBER 15

Attachment to Christ is the
only secret of detachment
from the world.

*I consider everything a loss compared to the surpassing
greatness of knowing Christ Jesus my Lord.*

PHILIPPIANS 3:8

APRIL 18

When tempted to lose patience with someone, stop and think how patient God has been with you.

Love is patient, love is kind.

I Corinthians 13:4

SEPTEMBER 14

Every child has a gift—but are we prepared to receive it?

Here is a boy with five small barley loaves and two small fish. ... Jesus then took the loaves, gave thanks, and distributed to those who were seated.

JOHN 6:9, 11

APRIL 19

God formed us; sin deformed us; but Christ
can transform us.

*All have sinned and fall short of the glory of God, and
are justified freely by his grace through the redemption
that came by Christ Jesus.*

ROMANS 3:23–24

SEPTEMBER 13

God allows us to be in darkness so he can
show us he is the Light.

*The people walking in darkness have seen
a great light.*

ISAIAH 9:2

APRIL 20

Jesus was God and man in one person, that
God and man might be happy together again.
George Whitfield

*God was pleased to have all his fullness dwell in Christ,
and through him to reconcile to himself all things ... by
making peace through his blood, shed on the cross.*

COLOSSIANS 1:19–20

SEPTEMBER 12

The answer always comes, but often in ways
you least expect.

*When I called, you answered me, O LORD; you made me
bold and stouthearted.*

PSALM 138:3

APRIL 21

Blessed is the soul who is too busy to worry during the day and too tired to worry at night.

When God gives any man wealth and possessions, and enables him to enjoy them, to accept his lot and be happy in his work—this is a gift of God. He seldom reflects on the days of his life, because God keeps him occupied with gladness of heart.

ECCLESIASTES 5:19–20

SEPTEMBER 11

Faith is not just believing that Christ Jesus can save, but trusting that he will.

Everyone who calls on the name of the Lord will be saved.

ROMANS 10:13

APRIL 22

Faith always takes the first step forward.

*The LORD had said to Abram, "Leave your country, your
people … go to the land
I will show you…." So Abram left, as the LORD had
told him.*

GENESIS 12:1, 4

SEPTEMBER 10

A man can only see his true self when he stands in the shadow of Christ.

Everything exposed by the light becomes visible, for it is light that makes everything visible. This is why it is said: "Wake up, O sleeper, rise from the dead, and Christ will shine on you."

EPHESIANS 5:13–14

APRIL 23

When you pray, it is better to have a heart without words, than words without heart.

The Spirit helps us in our weakness. We do not know what we ought to pray for, but the Spirit himself intercedes for us with groans that words cannot express.

ROMANS 8:26

SEPTEMBER 9

Man builds for a century; the Christian
builds for eternity.

*But one thing I do: forgetting what is behind and
straining toward what is ahead, I press on toward the goal
to win the prize for which God has called me heavenward.*

PHILIPPIANS 3:13–14

APRIL 24

Songs are heartbursts of gladness.

Therefore I will praise you, O LORD, among the nations;
I will sing praises to your name.

2 SAMUEL 22:50

SEPTEMBER 8

In his love God clothes us, enfolds us and
embraces us; that tender love completely
surrounds us, never to leave us.
Julian of Norwich

*The Lord ... will take great delight in you, he will quiet
you with his love, he will rejoice over you with singing.*
ZEPHANIAH 3:17

APRIL 25

The easiest way to keep temptation from growing is to nip it in the bud.

Watch and pray so that you will not fall into temptation. The spirit is willing, but the body is weak.

MARK 14:38

SEPTEMBER 7

Life without Christ–a hopeless end!
Life in Christ–endless hope!

*We wait for the blessed hope—the glorious appearing of
our great God and Savior, Jesus Christ.*

TITUS 2:13

APRIL 26

A man is tomorrow what he thinks today.

Set your minds on things above, not on earthly things.

COLOSSIANS 3:2

SEPTEMBER 6

If God sends us on stony paths, He will
provide us with strong shoes.
Alexander Maclaren

*The LORD is my strength and my shield; my heart trusts
in him, and I am helped.*

PSALM 28:7

APRIL 27

Our greatest glory is not in
never falling, but in rising every time we fall.

Humble yourselves before the Lord, and he will lift you up.

JAMES 4:10

SEPTEMBER 5

I am satisfied that when the Almighty wants
me to do or not to do any particular thing,
he finds a way of letting me know.
Abraham Lincoln

God is our God for ever and ever; he will be our guide
even to the end.

PSALM 48:14

APRIL 28

No condemnation now I dread.
Jesus, and all in him, is mine;
Alive in him, my living Head,
And clothed in righteousness Divine.
Charles Wesley

*The path of the righteous is like the first gleam of dawn,
shining ever brighter till the full light of day.*

PROVERBS 4:18

SEPTEMBER 4

Holy Spirit, think through me till your ideas
are my ideas.
Amy Carmichael

Whatever is true, whatever is noble, whatever is right, what-
ever is pure, whatever is lovely, whatever is admirable — if
anything is excellent or praiseworthy — think about these things.

PHILIPPIANS 4:8

APRIL 29

The Resurrection makes a difference—the difference between life and death, light and darkness, hope and despair.

God has given us new birth ... through the resurrection of Jesus Christ from the dead.

1 PETER 1:3

SEPTEMBER 3

Other books were given for information; the Bible was given for transformation.

You have been born again, not of perishable seed, but of imperishable, through the living and enduring word of God.

1 PETER 1:23

APRIL 30

Darkness cannot put out the Light; it can
only make him brighter.

*The light shines in the darkness, but the darkness has not
understood it.*

JOHN 1:5

SEPTEMBER 2

Sooner or later, all of us come to a "Red Sea" place in life.

The LORD drove the sea back ... and turned it into dry land ... and the Israelites went through the sea on dry ground.

EXODUS 14:21–22

MAY 1

Nature is an outstretched finger pointing toward God!

How many are your works, O LORD!

PSALM 104:24

SEPTEMBER 1

I love little children, and it is not a slight
thing when they who are fresh from God,
love us.
Charles Dickens

*Jesus said, "Let the little children come to me ... for the
kingdom of God belongs to such as these."*

MARK 10:14

MAY 2

As we learn to die to all around us, we can live for God above us.

Do not conform any longer to the pattern of this world, but be transformed by the renewing of your mind. Then you may be able to test and approve what God's will is.

ROMANS 12:2

AUGUST 31

Footprints in the sands of time can never be made by sitting down.

Jesus said, "Go into all the world and preach the good news to all creation. Whoever believes and is baptized will be saved."

MARK 16:15–16

MAY 3

Every believer should be a walking sermon.

Thanks be to God, who always leads in triumphal procession in Christ and through us spreads everywhere the fragrance of the knowledge of him.

2 CORINTHIANS 2:14

AUGUST 30

It is good to follow in the footsteps of a pastor who follows in the footprints of the Master.

If the LORD delights in a man's way, he makes his steps firm.

PSALM 37:23

MAY 4

Of all your worries, great or small, how many
of them never happened at all?

*Do not be anxious about anything, but in everything,
by prayer and petition, with thanksgiving, present your
requests to God.*

PHILIPPIANS 4:6

AUGUST 29

We often look too low for things that are
close by – look up instead!

My eyes are fixed on you,
O Sovereign LORD.

PSALM 141:8

MAY 5

One life can influence an entire community, just as a flower can fill a room with sweet perfume.

Those who are wise shall shine like the brightness of the heavens, and those who lead many to righteousness, like the stars for ever and ever.

DANIEL 12:3

AUGUST 28

Glorify the Lord more and the world will doubt him less.

Because your love is better than life, my lips will glorify you, O Lord. I will praise you as long as I live, and in your name I will lift up my hands.

PSALM 63:3–4

MAY 6

1 Cross + 3 Nails= 4 Given

Your sins have been forgiven on account of Christ's name.

1 John 2:12

AUGUST 27

A child is likely to see God as Father,
if they see God in their father.

*We will not hide them from their children; we will tell
the next generation the praiseworthy deeds of the LORD,
his power, and the wonders he has done.*

PSALM 78:

MAY 7

We shall rest and we shall see, we shall see and we shall love, we shall love and we shall pray, in the end which is no end.
St. Augustine

I heard what sounded like the roar of a great multitude in heaven shouting: "Hallelujah! Salvation and glory and power belong to our God."

REVELATION 19:1

AUGUST 26

Experience is what is left after
you make a mistake.

When pride comes, then comes disgrace,
but with humility comes wisdom.

PROVERBS 11:2

MAY 8

Don't be so concerned about working for
God that you overlook dwelling with God.

*I pray that ... Christ may dwell in your
hearts through faith.*

EPHESIANS 3:16–17

AUGUST 25

He who seeks the Father more than anything
He can give, is likely to have what he asks,
for he is not likely to ask amiss.
George Macdonald

God answered their prayers, because they trusted in him.

1 CHRONICLES 5:20

MAY 9

Every great and noble work seemed at first impossible.

Nothing is impossible with God.

LUKE 1:37

AUGUST 24

Faith is the vision of the heart.
It sees God even in the dark.

The righteous will live by faith.

ROMANS 1:17

MAY 10

Faith can never overdraw its account in the bank of Heaven.

If you have faith and do not doubt ... you can say to this mountain, "Go, throw yourself into the sea," and it will be done.

MATTHEW 21:21

AUGUST 23

The age of understanding and acceptance comes to different people at different times.

"Come now, and let us reason together" says the LORD.

ISAIAH 1:18

MAY 11

There is a feeling of eternity in youth.
William Hazlitt

Be happy, young man, while you are young, and let your heart give you joy.

ECCLESIASTES 11:9

AUGUST 22

Before you tell someone your troubles, take
time to listen to his.

Everyone should be quick to listen, slow to speak.

JAMES 1:19

MAY 12

Few things are impossible to diligence and skill. Great works are performed, not by strength, but perseverance.
Samuel Johnson

Blessed is the man who perseveres under trial, because when he has stood the test, he will receive the crown of life.

JAMES 1:12

AUGUST 21

The glory of God is a man fully alive.
Iranaeus

For as in Adam all die, so in Christ
all will be made alive.

1 CORINTHIANS 15:22

MAY 13

As we walk through the maze of life, we walk not alone, but hand in hand with another.

Come, let us go up to the mountain of the LORD. ...
He will teach us his ways, so that we may walk in his
paths.

ISAIAH 2:3

AUGUST 20

We all go through times when life seems to overwhelm us. The Bible reassures us that God's presence is with us to help us, even when we don't realize it.

M. F. Powers

The LORD said, "My Presence will go with you, and I will give you rest."

EXODUS 33:14

MAY 14

Faith sees the invisible, believes the incredible
and receives the impossible!

*This is the victory that has overcome the world,
even our faith.*

1 JOHN 5:4

AUGUST 19

If we want to increase in Christ, there must be a decrease of self.

We are God's workmanship, created in Christ Jesus to do good works, which God prepared in advance for us to do.

EPHESIANS 2:10

MAY 15

When the outlook is not good,
try the uplook.

*In my distress I called to the LORD, and he answered me.
... I called for help, and you listened to my cry.*

JONAH 2:2

AUGUST 18

Prayer does not need proof, it needs practice.

Your love is ever before me, Lord, and I walk continually in your truth.

PSALM 26:3

MAY 16

The wise man is also the just, the pious, the
upright, the man who walks in the
way of truth.
Otto Zockler

The wisdom that comes from heaven is first of all pure;
then peace-loving, considerate, submissive, full of mercy and
good fruit, impartial and sincere.

JAMES 3:17

AUGUST 17

Don't just count your years,
make your years count!
Dr. Ernest Meyers

*There is nothing better for men than to be happy and do
good while they live.*

ECCLESIASTES 3:12

MAY 17

No smile is so beautiful as the one that struggles through tears.

God will yet fill your mouth with laughter and your lips with shouts of joy.

JOB 8:21

AUGUST 16

No enemy is so near that God is not nearer.

*I will take refuge in the shadow of your wings until the
disaster has passed, O LORD.*

PSALM 57:1

MAY 18

Keep one thing forever in view—the truth;
though it may seem to lead you away from
the opinion of men, it will assuredly conduct
you to the throne of God.
Horace Mann

You will know the truth, and the truth will set you free.

JOHN 8:32

AUGUST 15

The God we worship writes his name
on our hearts.

*You show that you are a letter from Christ, ... written
not with ink but with the Spirit of the living God, not
on tablets of stone but on tablets of human hearts.*

2 CORINTHIANS 3:3

MAY 19

God is too good to be unkind and too wise to make mistakes.

The LORD God is a sun and shield; the LORD bestows favor and honor; no good thing does he withhold from those whose walk is blameless.

PSALM 84:11

AUGUST 14

Life's a voyage that's homeward bound.
Herman Melville

*In keeping with God's promise we are looking forward to
a new heaven and a new earth,
the home of righteousness.*

2 PETER 3:13

MAY 20

A well-read Bible is the sign of a well-fed soul.

*Like newborn babies, crave pure spiritual milk, so that
by it you may grow up in your salvation, now that you
have tasted that the Lord is good.*

1 PETER 2:2–3

AUGUST 13

Your greatest gift to others is a good example.
Dr. Geoffrey Still

Christ suffered for you, leaving you an example, that you should follow in his steps.

1 PETER 2:21

MAY 21

No one ever lost out by excessive
devotion to Christ.
H. A. Ironside

Jesus said, "By standing firm you will gain your life."

LUKE 21:19

AUGUST 12

The world's largest mission field begins just outside your door.

If you really keep the royal law found in Scripture, "Love your neighbor as yourself," you are doing right.

JAMES 2:8

MAY 22

The stops of a good man are ordered by the
Lord as well as his steps.

The Lord is good to those whose hope is in him.

LAMENTATIONS 3:25

AUGUST 11

We gain strength from temptations we resist.

No temptation has seized you except what is common to man. And God is faithful;. he will not let you be tempted beyond what you can bear.

1 CORINTHIANS 10:13

MAY 23

As soon as the soul begins to grow by the Spirit of God, it begins to live. In fact, as long as it continues in the Spirit it will never die.

The mind controlled by the Spirit is life and peace.

ROMANS 8:6

AUGUST 10

The final test of faith is not how much you believe, but how much you love.

Love the Lord your God with all your heart and with all your soul and with all your strength and with all your mind.

LUKE 10:27

MAY 24

In creation we see God's hand; in redemption
we see his heart.

Christ has appeared once for all ... to do away with sin
by the sacrifice of himself.

HEBREWS 9:26

AUGUST 9

When life writes "Ended" the angels write "Begun."

Jesus said, "He who believes in me will live, even though he dies."

JOHN 11:25

MAY 25

Prayer cuts knots you can't untie!

*When my life was ebbing away, I remembered you,
LORD, and my prayer rose to you, to your holy temple.*

JONAH 2:7

AUGUST 8

Encouragement costs you nothing to give,
but it is priceless to receive.

*Encourage one another and build each other up, just as
in fact you are doing.*

1 THESSALONIANS 5:11

MAY 26

Expect people to be better than they are; it
helps them to become better.
Merry Browne

In humility consider others better than yourselves.

PHILIPPIANS 2:3

AUGUST 7

No sorrow is too deep that God cannot feel it with us. And God wants to help deliver us from it.
M. F. Powers

O my Comforter in sorrow, my heart is faint within me.

JEREMIAH 8:18

MAY 27

Success lies not in what we start, but in what we finish.

Finish the work, so that your eager willingness to do it may be matched by your completion of it, according to your means. For if the willingness is there, the gift is acceptable according to what one has, not according to what he does not have.

2 CORINTHIANS 8:11–12

AUGUST 6

The Creator of the universe calls me his child! What a blessing! What a privilege! What a responsibility!
M. F. Powers

How great is the love the Father has lavished on us, that we should be called children of God! And that is what we are!

1 JOHN 3:1

MAY 28

Each one of us should keep a large cemetery in which to bury the faults of our friends.

Above all, love each other deeply, because love covers over a multitude of sins.

1 PETER 4:8

AUGUST 5

Those who are drawn towards Christ are
necessarily drawn towards each other.

*But if we walk in the light, as Christ is in the light, we
have fellowship with one another.*

1 JOHN 1:7

MAY 29

We are saved by atonement, not by attainment.

Command those who are rich in this present world ...
to put their hope in God, who richly provides us with
everything for our enjoyment.

1 TIMOTHY 6:17

AUGUST 4

They greatly dare who greatly trust.

When Daniel was lifted from the den, no wound was found on him, because he had trusted in his God.

DANIEL 6:23

MAY 30

Without encouragement, any one of us can lose confidence.

My purpose is that they may be encouraged in heart and united in love, so that they may have the full riches of complete understanding.

COLOSSIANS 2:2

AUGUST 3

No pain is so great that God does not bring
us comfort. And no situation is ever without
God's presence.
M. F. Powers

*Do not fear, for I am with you; do not be dismayed, for I
am your God. I will strengthen you and help you; I will
uphold you with my righteous right hand.*

ISAIAH 41:10

MAY 31

There is not a heart but has its moments of
longing, yearning for something better.
Henry Ward Beecher

*My soul faints with longing for your salvation, Lord, but
I have put my hope in your word.*

PSALM 119:81

AUGUST 2

Christ is not only a remedy for your weari-
ness and trouble, but he will give you an
abundance of the contrary, joy and delight.
Jonathan Edwards

*Jesus said, "I have come that they may have life, and
have it to the full."*

JOHN 10:10

JUNE 1

The truly happy person is one who still enjoys the scenery even when taking a detour.

Commit to the LORD whatever you do and your plans will succeed.

PROVERBS 16:3

AUGUST 1

You never get a second chance to make
a first impression.

Let your conversation be always full of grace.

COLOSSIANS 4:6

JUNE 2

There are two difficult things in life: making a name for yourself, and keeping it.

A good name is more desirable than great riches; to be esteemed is better than silver or gold.

PROVERBS 22:1

JULY 31

Each cross, each trouble has its day—then passes away.

Jesus said, "Heaven and earth will pass away, but my words will never pass away."

MATTHEW 24:35

JUNE 3

A joyful heart is the mark of one who has a
consistent walk with the Lord, who follows in
the footsteps of the Master.

M. F. Powers

*Teach me your way, O LORD, and I will walk in your
truth; give me an undivided heart, that I may
fear your name.*

PSALM 86:11

July 30

He who plants kindness gathers love.
St. Basil

He who sows righteousness reaps a sure reward.

Proverbs 11:18

JUNE 4

A kind heart is a fountain of gladness, making everything around it freshen into smiles.
Washington Irving

The mouth of the righteous is a fountain of life.

PROVERBS 10:11

JULY 29

The real measure of a person's wealth is what they have invested for eternity.

Where your treasure is, there your heart will be also.

LUKE 12:34

JUNE 5

When it comes to prayer, some people need a
faith lift.
Paula Powers

*Jesus said, "Whatever you ask for in prayer, believe that
you have received it, and it will be yours."*

MARK 11:23

JULY 28

Worry gives a small thing a big shadow.

When anxiety was great within me, your consolation brought joy to my soul, O Lord.

PSALM 94:19

JUNE 6

The Spirit breathes upon the Word,
And brings the truth to sight.
William Cowper

When he, the Spirit of truth, comes, he will guide you into all truth. He will not speak on his own; he will speak only what he hears, and he will tell you what is yet to come.

JOHN 16:13

JULY 27

God's grace: everything for nothing, when we don't deserve anything.

If, by the trespass of the one man, death reigned through that one man, how much more will those who receive God's abundant provision of grace and of the gift of righteousness reign in life through the one man, Jesus Christ.

ROMANS 5:17

JUNE 7

Great faithfulness is exhibited not so much in ability to do, as to suffer.

Jesus said, "Do not be afraid of what you are about to suffer. ... Be faithful, ... and I will give you the crown of life."

REVELATION 2:10

JULY 26

It's easier to pick a wise man by the things he doesn't say.

A man of knowledge uses words with restraint.

PROVERBS 17:27

JUNE 8

Never measure the mountain until you have
reached the top. It may not be as high
as it seems.

It is God who arms me with strength ... he
enables me to stand on the heights.

PSALM 18:32–33

JULY 25

Instead of counting your troubles, try adding
up your blessings!
Dr. Geoffrey Still

*Praise be to the God and Father of our Lord Jesus Christ,
who has blessed us in the heavenly realms with every
spiritual blessing in Christ.*

EPHESIANS 1:3

JUNE 9

Jesus started a fire upon the earth, and it is burning hot today, the fire of a new hope in the hearts of the hungry multitudes.
Frank C. Laubach

Set your hope fully on the grace to be given you when Jesus Christ is revealed.

1 PETER 1:13

July 24

Furnishings for your future home have all been sent on ahead.

[God has given us] an inheritance that can never perish, spoil or fade — kept in heaven for you.

1 Peter 1:4

JUNE 10

If you learn from losing, then you haven't lost.

He who listens to a life-giving rebuke will be at home among the wise.

PROVERBS 15:31

JULY 23

Music is the perfect way to express your love and devotion to God. It is one of the most magnificent and delightful presents God has given us.
Martin Luther

My heart is steadfast, O God; I will sing and make music with all my soul.

PSALM 108:1

JUNE 11

Faith is continuing to run, confident that you will get your "second wind."

In Christ, and through faith in him we may approach God with freedom and confidence.

EPHESIANS 3:12

JULY 22

There are times when God asks nothing of
His children except silence and patience.
Charles Seymour Robinson

Be still, and know that I am God.

PSALM 46:10

JUNE 12

It never matters how far apart we are—what
matters is how close we stay.
H. K. Barclay

*May the LORD keep watch between you and me when
we are away from each other.*

GENESIS 31:49

JULY 21

Like a river glorious is God's perfect peace,
Over all victorious in its bright increase.
Frances Ridley Havergal

The LORD gives strength to his people; the LORD blesses his people with peace.

PSALM 29:11

JUNE 13

There is a wideness in God's mercy
Like the wideness of the sea;
There's kindness in His justice
Which is more than liberty.
Frederick William Faber

I love the LORD, for he heard my voice; he heard my cry for mercy.

PSALM 116:1

JULY 20

You can be ready to live only if you are ready to die.
John & Betty Stamm, martyred missionaries

We … would prefer to be away from the body and at home with the Lord.

2 CORINTHIANS 5:8

JUNE 14

Wherever God rules over the human heart as
King, there is the kingdom of God established.
Paul W. Harrison

Jesus said, "The kingdom of God is within you."

LUKE 17:21

JULY 19

Of all the things you wear, your expression is the most important.

As water reflects a face, so a man's heart reflects the man.

PROVERBS 27:19

JUNE 15

I can't see the pattern into which each tangled thread is bent, but in trusting the Father, I am content.

I have learned to be content whatever the circumstances.

PHILIPPIANS 4:11

JULY 18

The word "joy" is too great and grand to be confused with the superficial things we call happiness. It was joy and peace which Jesus said he left men in his will.

Kirby Page

Jesus said, "I will see you again and you will rejoice, and no one will take away your joy."

JOHN 16:22

JUNE 16

There is more safety with Christ in the tempest than without Christ in the calm waters.

In the day of trouble God will keep me safe in his dwelling; he will hide me in the shelter of his tabernacle and set me high upon a rock.

PSALM 27:5

JULY 17

Cheer up! The Son hasn't gone out of business.

Arise, shine, for your light has come, and the glory of the LORD rises upon you.

Isaiah 60:1

JUNE 17

When we open our hearts to Jesus, God opens our minds to his Word.

Open my eyes that I may see wonderful things in your law, O Lord.

PSALM 119:18

JULY 16

Don't let your fears about the next hundred years discourage you from smiling now.

"Do not be afraid, for I am with you;
I will bless you," says the LORD.

GENESIS 26:24

JUNE 18

Courage is the anchor that holds one steady,
and enables one to climb on and on.

Be strong and take heart, all you who hope in the LORD.

PSALM 31:24

JULY 15

You can tell the mettle of a Christian when they rub against the world – the right kind will shine.

God will make your righteousness shine like the dawn, the justice of your cause like the noonday sun.

PSALM 37:6

JUNE 19

God's perfect will ... nothing more, nothing less, nothing else!

You need to persevere so that when you have done the will of God, you will receive what he has promised.

HEBREWS 10:36

JULY 14

Don't give from the bottom of the purse, but
from the bottom of the heart.

God loves a cheerful giver.

2 CORINTHIANS 9:7

JUNE 20

When you meet temptation, keep to the right!

Submit yourselves ... to God. Resist the devil, and he will flee from you. Come near to God and he will come near to you.

JAMES 4:7–8

JULY 13

It is not what men think of you, but what God knows of you that counts in the judgment.

We pray … that you may live a life worthy of the Lord and may please him in every way.

COLOSSIANS 1:10

JUNE 21

God passes through the thicket of the world,
and wherever his glance falls he turns all
things to beauty.
John of the Cross

*Flowers appear on the earth; the season of singing has
come, the cooing of doves is heard in our land.*

SONG OF SONGS 2:12

JULY 12

God has included you in his plans—have you
included him in yours?
Paul L. Powers

"I know the plans I have for you," declares the Lord, . . .
"plans to give you hope and a future."

JEREMIAH 29:11

JUNE 22

God has the film of my whole life in view, and not just the snapshot of my present existence.

"Before I formed you in the womb I knew you, before you were born I set you apart," says the LORD.

JEREMIAH 1:5

JULY 11

Scars for Christ today mean stars for Christ tomorrow!

Rejoice that you participate in the sufferings of Christ, so that you may be overjoyed when his glory is revealed.

1 PETER 4:13

JUNE 23

Feed your faith and starve your
doubt to death.
Paula Powers

Believe in the Lord Jesus, and you will be saved.

ACTS 16:31

JULY 10

Calvary restored mankind's lost inheritance.

God so loved the world that he gave is one and only Son, that whosoever believes in him shall not perish but have eternal life.

JOHN 3:16

JUNE 24

It is not the mere touching of the flower by the bee that gathers honey, but her abiding for a time on the flower that draws out the sweet.
Thomas Brooks

Jesus said, "I am the vine; you are the branches. If a man remains in me and I in him, he will bear much fruit."

JOHN 15:5

JULY 9

The man is a success who has lived well,
laughed often and loved much.
Robert Louis Stevenson

*LORD, who may dwell in your sanctuary? . . . He whose
walk is blameless and who does what is righteous, who
speaks the truth from his heart.*

PSALM 15:1–2

JUNE 25

The only safe and sure way to destroy
enemies is to make them your friends.

*Love your enemies, do good to them. . . . Then your
reward will be great, and you will be sons of the
Most High.*

LUKE 6:35

JULY 8

God is over all things, under all things,
outside all; within but not enclosed; without
but not excluded; wholly above, presiding,
wholly beneath, sustaining.
Hildebert of Lavardin

*You know when I sit and when I rise; you perceive my
thoughts from afar, O LORD.*

PSALM 139:2

JUNE 26

Cast all your cares on God; that anchor holds.
Alfred, Lord Tennyson

*Cast your cares on the Lord and he will sustain you; he
will never let the righteous fall.*

PSALM 55:22

JULY 7

God's gifts put man's best dreams to shame.
Elizabeth Barrett Browning

*Every good and perfect gift is from above, coming down
from the Father of the heavenly lights, who does not
change like shifting shadows.*

JAMES 1:17

JUNE 27

Turn to God for help in shaping your life–by prayer he will bring peace to the humblest.

"Like clay in the hand of the potter, so are you in my hand," says the LORD.

JEREMIAH 18:6

JULY 6

No service is fruitful, unless done in the
power of the Holy Spirit.

*The fruit of the Spirit is love, joy, peace, patience, kindness,
goodness, faithfulness, gentleness and self-control.*

GALATIANS 5:22–23

JUNE 28

God has never put anyone in a place too small to grow.

Wait for the Lord and keep to his way. He will exalt you to inherit the land.

PSALM 37:34

JULY 5

What you leave in your children should be more than what you leave to them.

A good man leaves an inheritance for his children's children.

PROVERBS 13:22

JUNE 29

The best way to live in the world is to live above it.

Jesus said, "You do not belong to the world, but I have chosen you out of the world."

JOHN 15:19

JULY 4

Only a free soul will never grow old!
Jean Paul Richter

It is for freedom that Christ has set us free.

GALATIANS 5:1

JUNE 30

If I could hear Christ praying for me in the next room, I would not fear a million enemies. Yet distance makes no difference. He is praying for me.
Robert M. McCheyne

Christ is able to save completely those who come to God through him, because he always lives to intercede for them.

HEBREWS 7:25

JULY 3

Put God first – be happy at last!

The LORD is the great God, the great King above all gods.

PSALM 95:3

JULY 1

Gold may bring beauty to the eye, but God's
Word brings beauty to the heart.

*I love your commands more than gold, more than pure
gold, O LORD.*

PSALM 119:127

JULY 2

Success in dealing with others is like making rhubarb pie: Use all the sweetener you can, then double it!

Pleasant words are a honeycomb, sweet to the soul and healing to the bones.

PROVERBS 16:24